S.O.A.R.

Dear Franklin,

With Best Wishes/

Roopak

S.O.A.R.

GROW FROM WITHIN AND UNLEASH
YOUR LIMITLESS POTENTIAL

Roopak Desai

ISBN: 173078609X
ISBN 13: 9781730786099
CreateSpace Independent Publishing Platform
North Charleston, SC

Printed in the United States of America

For my parents. I am because of them.

Contents

Acknowledgments

I AM GRATEFUL TO ALL the people who have come into my life at different points in the journey so far and who will come to it in the future—through a path of awakening and withstanding struggles. First and foremost, I am deeply indebted to Tanvi, my wife, who has been my pillar from the day we tied the knot. I would like to express my immense appreciation to her for staying by my side despite a roller-coaster ride I have sometimes put her through. I am ever thankful to my son, Aarush, for being a wonderful kid, who is growing up to be a smart and handsome young man, supporting his mom and staying focused at the same time. And I am and will always be thankful to God for blessing us with our lovely princess, Suhani, who is the cheer, laughter, and joy of my life.

I am extremely thankful to my brother, Vyapak, for his indispensable role in helping me fight depression, especially during the last episode where I was close to a nervous breakdown. I thank him for helping to lift my self-confidence by reminding me of the great things I have done thus far and the greater things I plan to do. I want to extend thanks to my dear friend and well-wisher, Giri Karuppusamy, who believed in me and helped me negotiate my anxiety attack very delicately at work few years ago. And, most importantly, my deepest regards to Will Lukang, my mentor, who stood by me again and again.

Finally, I would like to extend gratitude to all my dear friends who graciously agreed to be part of my book by providing me with the stories of their growth and journeys.

Introduction

"It's possible!"

My life's journey is a testament to these two golden words from Les Brown, an American motivational speaker who became known for saying it. My ultimate goal is to help empower people to rise and claim their destiny. That word, destiny, is often abstract and fuzzy. I am trying to make it less fuzzy. With this in mind, this book offers a compilation of eighteen awakening moments and experiences that gradually led to my transformation and rebirth via rituals, spiritual practices, lessons, teachings, and what I can only describe as undeniable blessings from the Almighty. I was slowly introduced to the new version of myself. Once I met "him" I realized he was not only a better version of me but one filled with limitless potential.

I was in Stamford, Connecticut, on a professional training in June 2017. One day, the day was beautiful, and I felt like going to the shore for a walk in the evening. Upon reaching Cummings Park Beach, the closest beach, I realized it was closed. Did I get disheartened? Did I curse my fate? Did I blame myself for not checking if the beach was going to be open or not? No, I did not allow any of those self-depleting behaviors or thoughts to ruin my present moment. Instead, I thought, *So what? This is not the end of the world. It happens, and that's life!* "We all are given lemons in our lives. It is about making lemon juice from it and enjoying being and living." Immediately, I decided to go to another nearby West Beach and felt no restriction in trying to reach them, so, sure enough, I found another stunningly beautiful beach with lovely surroundings. In the middle of a small island, where a few boats were moored to the pier, there was a charming little house projecting serenity I did not expect to find at that moment. This was the picture of my dreams, sitting there and waiting to be claimed as my sanctuary. I immediately thanked God for having led me to this beach. It inspired me to pen down preface of this book the very morning. How many of us take the steps our heart tells us to consider? How many of us really follow our dreams and take steps to bring them to realize and achieve them? How many of us genuinely go within to search for what we are about, why we are here, and what we want to be? This book is about finding answers to these questions, about exploring the process of realizing our dreams— how to grow from within and realize our true potential.

How many of us truly believe in ourselves and pursue our dreams until they become a reality? Our first instinct is to ask our minds before doing something whether it is worth taking a chance. Taking a chance requires us to get out of our comfort zones. The mind protects itself first due to the fear of failing. In other words, egoistic tendencies keep us from exploring the unknown. That is how most of us live our lives. We never truly realize our potential and accomplish something that the heart and soul long for. And it is not our fault. This is how society expects us to live. Whether taught by our parents or teachers, the default path is to have a good education, get a good job, earn a good living, marry a good spouse, have good children, keep working hard to support the family, and retire. In the meantime, it is our children's turn to do the same and so on. This is absolutely fine. There is nothing wrong or right about it. But did you ever ask yourself if this is what you are here for? Have you ever truly listened to your heart to find your inner calling and, once you did, committed to building what is needed to go above and beyond your limiting beliefs and society-driven values?

Do not despair. Everyone in this world is different, and every lifestyle is different. Some people figure out while they are growing up what their true passions are and follow their hearts right away. And then there are people who take some time to go through life's experiences until one day when they inquire about the true meaning of life and their inner calling. Take my example; it took twenty years for me to discover myself and the inner world inside of me. This world is limitless. Your potential is limitless. Once the opportunity arises and one is awakened, that is the time to rise and go for it, shedding all doubts and fear to work on yourself and claim your destiny. It is like being a larva in a cocoon during metamorphosis. The caterpillar does not stop its efforts while growing. It keeps working on itself during the growth process and soon turns out to be a beautiful butterfly. You have to act with courage during defining moments, make tough decisions, and go out to explore the world that is calling for you.

My brother Vyapak made some of his toughest decisions out of courage and what his heart told him while he was growing up. First, he took up commerce instead of continuing in science for his studies in eleventh grade because he realized that he did not have any interest in the field of science and wanted to pursue commerce. He listened to his heart and made a bold move. Later, he withstood a significant setback of not clearing the final examination for Chartered Account certification despite three tries. He did not succumb to these failures but wisely marched forward with his degree and completed Masters in law. He found his niche in practicing law and was highly successful practicing in the High Court of Gujarat. He then took an enterprising step to move to Mumbai for his career growth. These decisions and the urge to pursue his heart's calling weren't easy. They were the most difficult times, but now a phenomenal lawyer at the international level who is well recognized in his field of expertise. This happened because he went out of his comfort zone when it was time to follow his dreams. We often see people's immediate successes but don't realize what exactly went into it and the process they had to go through for achieving this success. Success is not something you pursue; it is something you attract with your qualities and self-effort and by relentlessly following your heart and passion.

You have everything that you need to achieve a fulfilling, successful life and live your real potential. Like a butterfly in its metamorphosis, you have to keep striving, building up courage and confidence. There are multiple streams of thought and action that contribute toward our self-actualization. This book is my attempt to put them all together, as well as to provide my teaching and experiences based on realizations gleaned from interviews from many accomplished people who have achieved greatness.

My recommendation is that you don't rush through reading this book in one sitting. Instead, read one chapter a week. Stop to reflect upon what you think of the virtue conveyed in each chapter. Note down the motivation to take away to incorporate in your daily life. Apply it. Observe what happens. And then move on to the next chapter. I wish you all the best for your journey of the self-discovery and unpredictable growth.

Find Passion and Purpose

You have to know who you are to grow to your potential. But
you have to grow first in order to know who you are.

—*JOHN MAXWELL, AUTHOR, SPEAKER*

LIFE IS A JOURNEY, AND until you determine your destination, you are just a wanderer without any vision or mission. It all starts by asking a few basic questions and continuing to inquire until you find the answers for yourself.

1. Who are you?
2. Where have you come from and where are you going?
3. What do you want to become?
4. Why are you here?
5. How do you want to use your gifts and abilities to impact the world?

The first and principal response to these questions is to know your passion and commit to following it. While living your day-to-day life, have you ever asked yourself what drives you? The majority of us seeks financial security, even wealth for some, but is that all? What about love, happiness, security, being successful, support, family, and attaining spiritual oneness with oneself?

What is that drives you? What does a driven person do to keep sharpening their skills and continue building on their abilities to achieve their dreams?

It is passion. Yes, unless you have figured out what your real passion is, you are just existing and being a passive participant in the precious gift of life you have received. Why would you want to do that and not live the life of your dreams? The choice is always yours: either to change for the greater good or to stay what you are by living in your comfort zone with wishful thoughts and dreams. To discover your passion, you first have to find out who you are. What do you like to do? What are your abilities and skills? What makes you happy? Deep down in your soul, what do you care about and want to do? Discovering yourself and your passion is the same process. Once you find out this passion, you learn how to master it, make it a habit, and follow it with dedication. You essentially become the passion that is worth living for.

A dream without a vision is merely a wish. Likewise, passion, if not directed for a specific purpose, lacks the impetus we need to achieve it. Finding your purpose is of vital importance. Living life is one thing, but living a purposeful life is the answer to having a meaning and flow in life. Finding out your purpose from within will lead to you contributing your skills and abilities to society in the most meaningful and fulfilling way for all. Once you have discovered your passion and purpose, its vision will fuel the energy you will need to accomplish your mission to the fullest of your potential.

For the longest time, I drifted in the wind. I hadn't identified my passion, my true purpose for being. It was not until five years ago that I had my first wake-up call after coming out of one of the most severe attacks of anxiety and depression I had ever experienced. I had been suffering from chronic anxiety and depression for the twenty-five years and lived a mediocre life with self-doubts, living in the past and blaming fate for everything. I didn't take ownership or responsibility for my thoughts and actions. Was I doing the right thing? Not really. Did I not give control and power to others? Yes, I did.

Regardless of your state of mind, individual situation, and limitation, it is up to you to take control of and be in charge of your life, isn't it? Coming out of the mental trap of living in self-pity and deciding to live with a twinkle or spark in your eyes for doing what you love, desire, aspire for, and dream of is in your hands.

Luckily, I took that bold step. I decided to let go of my past and begin the new life of my choice. I decided to take a leap of faith and start doing the things that my heart told me to do. I rebuilt my life on a foundation of self-belief and ownership. I decided to stop feeding on self-doubts, weaknesses, and starving for the sympathy of others. I came out of the inquiry mode and awakened one day to take up running. I started from zero to now becoming a "MarathonForLife" runner. I found my passion for running and continued to harness it and take on life as an adventure. I figured out my sole purpose in life is to positively impact the lives of millions and enable them to achieve good health and 24-7 happiness and well-being.

As I reflect on my journey of the past five years, I realize that it was my relentless search for my passion that got me to where I am today, against all the odds. I centered my life on my desire deep down to seek and discover what I genuinely like and enjoy doing and then follow it as a ritual, thus leading a purposeful life with my full potential.

In 2016, although I had registered for the TCS Amsterdam Marathon, twelve weeks before the event, I was in no position to run. I was set back by another episode of anxiety and depression. But this time I made sure to keep running no matter how much my mind's weaknesses pulled me back. I persisted in my efforts to prepare clinically and mentally for the marathon and was ready within ten weeks just by holding on to my passion for running. I was not only able to overcome the anxiety and depression attack but also finish the marathon with one of my best times. The key lesson I learned was that when you follow your passion and strive hard for the purpose, then the whole universe helps you to achieve your goals and dreams.

TIME TO GET INSPIRED:

Sparsh Shah: He who wants to SPARSH (touch) millions of lives one at a time

Sparsh Shah, a 14-year-old singing prodigy who lives in the US, was born with almost 40 fractures. He was born with a life-threatening genetic condition called orthogenesis imperfecta. This condition makes his bones extremely fragile and brittle – even a hard handshake can break his bones. He cannot bear weight on his hands and legs, so he cannot walk or run like other normal kids. He has had more than 125 fractures in the first 12 years of his life already, and the doctors cannot predict how many more are to come. Against all the odds, he fought from the day he was born, and with the faith of his parents, he grew into a strong person with passion, dreams, and vision. Sparsh started learning Indian classical music at the age of 6 and is a student of Pandit Jasraj Institute of Music (PJIM) since 2009. He also learns American vocal music. In April 2015, Sparsh participated in and won the prestigious talent competition Young Voice of NYC, and was honored to be made the 'Youth Ambassador' for St. Jude Children's Research Hospital. He now supports the hospital in spreading awareness about the fight against pediatric cancer.

Last year, he went through one of the toughest times with the experience of spinal cord fusion surgery, which left him in excruciating pain and unbearable nausea— broken, in a literal sense. But that did not deter him from his calling, and he came out stronger with these three beliefs:

1. A person's true courage is the ability to cry and smile at the time of adversity since pain is inevitable, but suffering is optional.
2. Fight for good. We have the power to choose the path of greatness.
3. Have tremendous faith and draw upon the higher powers to seek help when left with nothing.

He found passion in music and made a mission to touch the lives of millions by being an example of courage, hard work, and success. He unleashed a limitless potential for himself and for those to whom he is an inspiring role model. In living his passion for a purpose to his full potential, he has already performed over eighty live performances and has received many awards at the age of thirteen. Despite all the challenges he has faced, Sparsh's spirit is unbreakable. He dreamed to singing in front of a billion people one day which came true recently when he performed in the grand finale of *Kaun Banega Crorepati*, a Sony Television Show hosted by the Amitabh Bachchan, the legend of the Indian Film Industry.

He makes the following suggestion to live with passion and purpose:

"Dream big. Have a mission because with mission comes the vision. Have a map, work hard, and find out how you are going to reach your destination. Success is the journey, and you must endeavor to achieve greatness."

TIME TO REFLECT

—

THINKING ABOUT THIS CHAPTER, WHAT DID YOU
LEARN? WHAT CAN YOU APPLY IN YOUR LIFE?

MOTIVATE

———

WHAT MOTIVATION DO YOU FEEL STIRRING INSIDE OF YOU? WHAT'S ONE STEP YOU CAN TAKE TOWARDS NURTURING THAT FEELING OF CHANGE?

What is your Why?

*'Why' is how you explain your purpose and the
reason you exist and behave as you do!*

—SIMON SINEK

THE "WHY" FOR YOUR BEING is the core engine that connects your passion and potential to achieve your dreams and leads you to the pinnacle of success with the universe supporting you at every turn. In other words, your passion will help you in finding your *why*. Why are you here? Why are you doing what you are doing? How can you contribute to others with your passions and abilities? Finally, having identified your purpose, get your engine to go ahead with all its capacity to wherever the universe takes you for you to be a part of your life's dreams and mission.

In a powerful TED talk by Tony Robbins entitled "What is your why," Robbins focuses on finding out the following three things for yourself:

1. What gives you fulfillment?
2. What is your passion?
3. What drives you?

The decision you make as to what you want to make of your life and *why,* shapes your destiny. It amounts to the fact that Robbins shares based on his interactions with over three million people over a period of thirty years of work. Emotions that are created based on this *why* sets you in motion.

We are always on the lookout for motivation to change something in our lives or to bring some new thing in our lives. But eventually, we either get distracted or derailed from the goal—or leave midway without seeing it through the end. The main reason is that it is not about your motivation but your motive. You can be motivated to do different things, but it is a motive that leads to your end goal. In other words, once you discover the *why* then motivation follows. You need to feel the urge to grow and be something more than you are at present.

The evidence to why this is important, for me, comes from seeing how discovering this *why* has transformed my sedentary life. I found my source of fulfillment is making a positive difference in the lives of people. My passion is running and a healthy lifestyle, which keeps me motivated and staying positive. I continuously aim to improve myself in every area of life to reach and utilize my full potential along the way. I now totally believe that out of all the physical, psychological, and emotional needs of a human being, to live a fulfilled life, you need to know your *why* for your actions and decisions.

Once you have clarity about your *why* and take your decisions accordingly, you become the owner of your destiny. It makes you unstoppable and fearless to pursue your goals, dreams, and vision—fulfilling your purpose.

TIME TO GET INSPIRED:
Mel Robbins: The author of *The 5 Seconds Rule*

Mel Robbins was in shambles with everything falling apart in her personal life, marriage, and family. And points came where she felt utterly powerless and out of control. She was always on the lookout for a force within to turn things around, take charge, and put the past behind her. Her *why* was to take charge of her life and to tackle adversities by achieving physical, emotional, and spiritual balance. A moment came when she realized the formula is as simple as it sounds—to begin counting backward 5, 4, 3, 2, 1 and then go, which brought an end to her misery and suffering. She used this formula to get herself out of her bed to take care of all the tasks and goals she intended. She used it to get out of bed at 5:00 a.m. every day, to work out for physical well-being, for meditation practice for her spiritual nourishment, and finally to focus on schedule for emotional well-being and feel in control of day—all with the same five-second rule. The rule is simple: The moment you have an instinct to act on a goal you must work on it immediately or within five seconds, otherwise, your mind will start leaning towards procrastination. This technique lets your brain eliminate doubts, fears, and emotions that hinder you from performing. She turned not only her life around but wrote an international best-selling book, *The 5 Seconds Rule.* Robbins presses hard on the fact that the drive has to come from within to do something and to be something.

TIME TO REFLECT

THINKING ABOUT THIS CHAPTER, WHAT DID YOU
LEARN? WHAT CAN YOU APPLY IN YOUR LIFE?

MOTIVATE

WHAT MOTIVATION DO YOU FEEL STIRRING INSIDE OF
YOU? WHAT'S ONE STEP YOU CAN TAKE TOWARDS
NURTURING THAT FEELING OF CHANGE?

AWAKENING 3

What are your Idols and Values?

If you want to become oak, then you need to think like an acorn.

—UNKNOWN

WHAT TYPE OF PERSON DO you want to become? If you ask this question to yourself every day, it makes you stay in inquiry mode for quite some time. It will lead to the formation of specific impressions in your brain for the ideals you are nurturing. It then results in self-actualization by you starting to work on cultivating your values to become the person you want to be. It is a journey—and a fascinating one. It all boils down to the values you carry, hold, and nourish. It is about who you look up to; to become the person you aspire to be.

I have learned that there are three ways that you can approach living life:

1. Looking down: Lead by example and pull someone up.
2. Looking sideways: Lead by joining hands.
3. Looking up: Lead by looking up to your idols who have already achieved greatness and working on a living, nurturing, and developing those values.

It is on you to decide how you want to lead your life. Once you recognize the role models you want to look up to; the churn starts happening inside you as part of self-actualization. You end up doing self-introspection as part of the discovery process. As you go deeper inside yourself, you will start figuring out who you are, why you are here, what you are here for, and what you want to be.

I underwent the same process of self-discovery. After being in inquiry for almost twenty years, things started becoming more apparent to me while recovering from my anxiety and depression attack five years ago that was close to a nervous breakdown. It was time for the curtain to be raised to identify my idols to look up to and the related values that I want to build upon. My idols and values thus became my guiding torch, and it took daily practices to keep harnessing them. I happen to see myself looking up to six idols who gave me a much-warranted impetus to focus and grow into a greater human being full of passion, purpose, meaning, and values.

Here are my six role models that I look up to the most:

1. **Amitabh Bachchan:** A legendary actor who has ruled the Indian movie industry now for more than fifty years. The values that I look up to him for are: character, work ethic, family values, integrity, and humility.
2. **Mahatma Gandhi:** The father of India who was instrumental in leading the country to freedom by fighting the British rule with non-violence resistance. The values that I look up to him for are courage, endurance, and fearlessness.
3. **Richard Branson:** A dyslexic boy who turned into a most influential and successful entrepreneur. The values that I look up to him for are: forerunner and self-believer.
4. **Virat Kohli:** The prolific Indian batsman and the captain of the Indian national cricket team. The values that I look up to him for are Lionheart, self-pride, and commitment.
5. **Milind Soman:** A heartthrob model, philanthropist, and a running champion having run numerous marathons and ultra-marathons.

An icon for health and wellness, the values that I look up to him for are perseverance, zealousness, and vitality.

6. **Sri Sri Ravi Shankar:** The founder of Art of Living. He is my spiritual guru.

Who are your idols? What values are significant to you for building into your life?

If you take an example of one of my idols, every time I get up and get ready for running, I think about Milind Soman. I think about his passion for running and his dedication to serving others by motivating people to live a healthier life. When I am running, I see him with my mind's eye. I see his mindful running style and him being in flow and in full control in his running form. I had the privilege of meeting him in person as well. By looking up to him, it motivates me to become stronger and leaner thus becoming the person I want to be. I came to realize that who you want to become is all inside you. The key is that you have to think like the person you want to be.

So the question is why are values and idols the cornerstones for becoming the person you want to be? They are the templates or blueprints, through which your platform is built for living a successful and fulfilling life. They are your GPS for guiding you on the path for doing things that you are passionate about and lead a purposeful and meaningful life.

Without values or not having someone to look up to, you will end up being mediocre and can go astray. It is next to impossible to be able to reach your limitless potential while growing from within without identifying what values you want to live by.

TIME TO GET INSPIRED:
Tawanda Gladman: Achiever of fulfilling success

Tawanda was born and brought up in a well-to-do, loving, and large family. Right from a very early age, she realized and felt the importance of discipline and being a person that one would like an honor. Her US

Air Force training during post-high school years laid the foundation of values she carries thus far: integrity, teamwork, and to do things to the best of her abilities.

She went through tough and divisive times when choosing between a well-paid corporate career with growth opportunities and something that her heart beckoned her to do. She went with what aligned with her natural interest and got into a fulfilling profession in the field of cosmetics, becoming a beautician/hair stylist. She made a prudent choice to go in the direction of her heart. She shared her dreams with her family who helped her gain emotional support. With limited resources, lots of hard work, and disciplined efforts, she completed her license as a cosmetologist while doing her job, studies, and practical training.

Now she is a full-time hairstylist and believes that the sky now is the limit for her to grow and live up to her full potential. She thinks that her values that were cultivated during her very young age and which she kept honing led her to a place where she felt fulfilled, happy, and ready to take on new challenges to grow and unleash her limitless potential.

She makes the following suggestion for having idols and values:

"The one thing that differentiates from living a fulfilling life to that of being mediocre is to keep your head high and be grounded at the same time with the foundation of your values, determination, and disciplined efforts. And that is indeed the way to lead successfully in the direction of your dreams."

TIME TO REFLECT

THINKING ABOUT THIS CHAPTER, WHAT DID YOU
LEARN? WHAT CAN YOU APPLY IN YOUR LIFE?

MOTIVATE

___

WHAT MOTIVATION DO YOU FEEL STIRRING INSIDE OF YOU? WHAT'S ONE STEP YOU CAN TAKE TOWARDS NURTURING THAT FEELING OF CHANGE?

Be Kind

Be the rainbow in someone's cloud.

—*Maya Angelou*

Have you ever given a thought as to how another person would feel just by you being there or doing something for him or her selflessly? What would change for you and the other person? To be kind is more important than to sympathize or advise. Many times you don't need a brilliant mind to speak but need a kind heart to listen and give.

Let me share a story that touched my heart. There was once a person named Karsanbhai a few decades ago. He was well off, and he started helping others anonymously. As per his practice, every month he would hand over an envelope of $1,000 to any person whom he met on the way while on his daily evening walk.

In the same neighborhood, there was a person named Chandanbhai. He was a very down-to-earth person, and he recently had gone through some money crunch and was in debt for $50,000. Being a man of integrity and known for paying off his debts, he was scrambling for the last $5,000 for three months which he had promised to give back to the lender on a particular day. After his final efforts, he was still $1,000 short and was very sad. On the evening before the day he had committed to give the last payment of his debt, he had given up all hope and went for a walk to get some air. It so happened that Karsanbhai bumped into him out of nowhere, and Chandanbhai lost his balance. Karsanbhai exchanged greetings with the stranger and pulled out the envelope to give it to him. Chandanbhai was surprised and questioned why and asked what was in it. Karsanbhai simply said, "You open it after you reach home," and kept walking. Perplexed, Chandanbhai had no clue what to do and continued walking. After reaching home and opening the envelope, he was moved to tears when he found $1,000. And he was full of gratefulness for this miracle.

Was this a miracle? Was Karsanbhai a messenger from God? Was this God's gift for Chandanbhai's good deeds and his integrity? Or was it a simple random act of kindness?

Kindness is a thoughtful feeling or an act that shows that other people matter. It is about being a person who makes other people feel special. It is a gesture of love and cares for others. It is compassion for others, a spontaneous and a conscious act of doing well for others.

The positive effects of kindness are experienced in the brain of everyone who does the act of kindness, receiver of compassion, and witness for it. Kindness is a beautiful way of reaching out to a weary heart and making it shine like a rising sun. It's like weight-training with the difference that with that an act of kindness you build up your compassion "muscle." You feel blessed and are inspired to pay it forward on receiving an act of kindness. You can make a positive impact in the lives of others and in turn to yourself just by a mindful thought, gesture, or action. Isn't that wonderful?

TIME TO GET INSPIRED:
Nadya Zilov: A lovely lady with the kindest heart!

Her journey started by being a coach at Dale Carnegie Program in 2009. According to her, her life-changing event was in 2012 in the form of a Tony Robbins seminar. After witnessing a walk on fire by participants like her, her beliefs were transformed entirely. It was a revelation to her that fear is not outside but inside your brain. She continued to do amazing things that she had always wanted to do but was afraid to do. Recently, she pioneered a mindfulness program in the Bank of America.

But her growth from within and the unleashing of her potential did not happen overnight. She faced the scariest moment of her life when she realized that her rheumatoid arthritis was progressing very fast; there were days in 2015 when she could not walk in the morning. But her mantra became "I do not know how I will feel, but I can trust this pain and embrace it" to change her through the process of overcoming fear. And on being committed to her well-being, she has now reversed her arthritis and is proud to be in the best physical shape that she's been in the last ten years. She was able to transition naturally by accepting her condition, loving herself and others without judgment, and being kind to anyone and everyone who came into her life.

She is the messenger of kindness—and being kind to herself is equally important to her. She is a strong advocate of love. She believes that we should love ourselves the way we are and we are not. If we love and accept our ugliness, we can open up and create a space for love.

She makes the following suggestion for being a compassionate person:

"If we love and accept ourselves fully, we will not be judging and evaluating people around us, and we will not be negatively triggered as much in our lives. If the love is present, then we will be focusing much less on material things, because all material things are just cravings to be loved and to be comfortable with ourselves."

TIME TO REFLECT

———

THINKING ABOUT THIS CHAPTER, WHAT DID YOU
LEARN? WHAT CAN YOU APPLY IN YOUR LIFE?

MOTIVATE

WHAT MOTIVATION DO YOU FEEL STIRRING INSIDE OF
YOU? WHAT'S ONE STEP YOU CAN TAKE TOWARDS
NURTURING THAT FEELING OF CHANGE?

Be Patient and Persevere

Let us be up and doing, with a heart for any fate,
Keep achieving, keep pursuing, and learn to labor and to wait,
And get crowned to be a winner at the end.

—UNKNOWN

SUCCESS IS NEVER ACHIEVED LINEARLY. It goes through a curvy, bumpy, and spirally rides. What it takes is "sadhana" (meaning disciplined and dedicated practice) to sail through the roller-coaster ride and come out at the top instead of being buried under the weight of doubt, fear, and self-limiting beliefs. It requires patience and perseverance through the process and consistency in efforts to taste the sweetness of the success.

When you are pushing yourself to the limit, you are going to face three things. First, there will be a struggle. Second, you will be met with failure and will most likely feel like quitting. And third and finally, you will taste victory. But the only thing that matters is the winner's attitude that you should have while going through each of these phases.

1. The struggle phase—the antidote is patience.
The struggle will help you uncover your strength. It's the best way of figuring out who we indeed are and what we're truly capable of. When we are faced with constant adversity, we can either let that struggle define

us keeping us away from reaching our potential or we can use that struggle as motivation to get better and improve. What is important is to have patience and continue the efforts with faith in the resolve and capabilities bestowed inside us. The most worthy examples that I can cite are of Mahatma Gandhi, who, following his doctrine of nonviolence movement (Satyagraha) helped attain freedom for India after 250 years of British rule, and Nelson Mandela, a South African leader who spent 27 years in prison for opposing apartheid. Upon his release from prison, Mandela became the first president of a black-majority-ruled South Africa in which apartheid was officially ended. A symbol of hope for many, Mandela is also a former winner of the Nobel Peace Prize.

2. The failure phase—the antidote is perseverance through the process. You are bound to encounter disappointments, and those are the testing times. Failure is our greatest teacher. It takes you through the lessons that you need to learn to keep climbing higher up the ladder of success. Failure shows you precisely what to do differently. It's a blessing in disguise, and it's inevitable—so embrace it. What is essential is to persevere through the process while keeping your vision and goal in mind.

3. The victory phase—the goal realized.
Finally, the goal is realized for the one who stays consistent in his or her endeavors. Never give in to criticisms directed towards your struggles or failures. You may improvise the direction but not the destination. Victory will remind you it was worth it. It's promised, as long as you're willing to put in the work. You see, success can only happen when you've conquered that struggle and accepted that failure.

To become your best and reach greatness, you need to break free of your comfort zone. You need to challenge yourself, reinvent the way you think—one step at a time, one day at a time, to bring out your best self through adversities, struggles, and failures and be victorious. The best news of all is that you don't have to wait to do this. You can start right now.

Let me share a story. It is the story of a guy who never ran a mile, never thought of running, and never dreamt of running a marathon, but went on to run his first half marathon in November 2013.

It all started on December 25, 2012, when he decided to stop being a couch potato and do something for his mind and body to a make a difference for himself. He started running with baby steps. Every day at 6:00 a.m. sharp, he put on his shoes to get on the road and practiced running irrespective of rain, sunshine, or snow.

He started training with the podcast for 5k101, a ten-week program to get ready for a 5K. Months later he ran his 5K race on April 7, 2013. And he went ahead to register for the Philadelphia half marathon. It is the training of mind and body to endure pain and fatigue. As per him, "One thing I learned is once you make a resolve and commit to it, the universe comes to your help for its manifestation."

On the day of the marathon, there was only one goal, and that was to cross the finish line. Though in excruciating pain in the right knee by the tenth mile, he kept running and completed the marathon with a strong sense of pride, saying, "I am what I am supposed to be and have everything in me to become what I want to be."

Guess whose story is it? Yes, it's about me, a story of me being patient, perseverant, and consistent. And I'm now proud to have the "MarathonForLife" runner title. I went on to run a few half marathons and have run four full marathons—including the NYC Marathon twice!

I have come to believe that if you want to change your life, start by changing your behavior, and make the new behavior something you follow through consistently. Success is not guaranteed to come at your time; you need to persevere, struggle, overcome failures, learn from the process, and stay patient to taste victory.

TIME TO GET INSPIRED:

Chris Connor: Author of *Values of You - The Guide to Living Boldly and Joyfully Through the Power of Core Values*

After interviewing Connor, it became crystal clear to me that for achieving any goal one needs to persevere and be patient to kiss the victory. He was no exception. Connor figured it out for himself while dating his now loving wife. He had broken up with her, his then-girlfriend, but did not give up. He kept patience and continued growing through adversity, developing strong values and character. He persevered through the process while being consistent in his efforts. He later approached her again and they are now a happily married couple.

The lesson learned from the recovery of his crisis of losing his fiancée that he truly loved and courting her back by building strong character and bringing discipline in his life helped him to negotiate adversities faced in his professional career as well. His positive attitude, disciplined approach and faith in himself helped him not only to negotiate loss of a job but also converted it into an opportunity to fulfill his desire to write a book *Values of You*, which he completed recently.

He makes the following suggestion for being patient and persevering:

"The secret to success is having dedication and focus, going all in with a plan of action and hard work with a positive attitude. And the mantra or adage of his life: *Attitude + Effort = Success.*"

TIME TO REFLECT

THINKING ABOUT THIS CHAPTER, WHAT DID YOU
LEARN? WHAT CAN YOU APPLY IN YOUR LIFE?

MOTIVATE

—

WHAT MOTIVATION DO YOU FEEL STIRRING INSIDE OF YOU? WHAT'S ONE STEP YOU CAN TAKE TOWARDS NURTURING THAT FEELING OF CHANGE?

Decision to Change

I am the master of my fate; I am the captain of my soul.

—*William Henley*

THIS QUOTE IS ONE OF the most significant and profound truths that Henley shared. What he's saying is that it is up to us to make choices and implement the necessary changes to meet with success. There may be many pathways, but the goal is the same: to be happy and achieve greatness. Your choice of a particular path is an individual matter and related to your will. You are free to choose the way that best suits you.

In this process, it is vital that you engage in an internal search and find out what feels right, according to your inner conscience. You cannot give your very best unless you have the right conditions for it to be manifested. You need to feel you have the right conditions so that you can do things joyfully, and fully express your highest purpose in life. In this process, you become aware of what brings you inner joy. Once you become aware of it, you'll be able to live your life in true peace and love.

From moment to moment, things are moving and changing. We can accept these changes or reject them, but regardless of our personal choices, this process is beyond our control. Change takes place on two levels: it occurs both inside and outside of us. The changes that happen inside are caused by what we see and as a result of our experiences with the outside world. And how we feel inside is the result of our personal choices of thoughts and actions and most importantly how we perceive the world around us.

Therefore, it's vital to be conscious of the changes that take place inside of us in the first place and then to develop a level of awareness that allows us to experience the outside world from a space of true personal power. It enables us to become creators of our reality and to achieve personal greatness.

Until five years ago, I've lived life in complete disconnection with my inner self. I was not myself and lived according to other people's projections of reality. Due to this dysfunctional dynamic that started when I was a teenager, I suffered various episodes of anxiety and depression throughout the years. However, in December of 2012, I had a real breakthrough. During the recovery period from a major depressive and anxiety attack in which I was near a breakdown, I got an awakening glimpse of what would change my life. I started to run, and through that new decisive activity, I was able to take control of my life, my thoughts, my beliefs and become accountable for who I am. Running nurtures and nourishes my mind, body, and spirit. And it provides me with immense joy and a unique sense of freedom. After all that I have been through, I have learned some valuable lessons about the wisdom of life and how to navigate from an empowered space. Regardless of external circumstances, I know now that I have the power to change my mindset and take more control of my life.

Zig Ziglar's quote exemplifies wonderfully how I now choose to live my life: "You are what you are and where you are because what has gone into your mind. You can change what you are and where you are by changing what goes into your mind."

TIME TO GET INSPIRED:
Susie Verde: Transformation through choosing to live to a higher calling

Verde is a native Brazilian and presently living in New York City. During her life, she was faced with some life-altering events that prompted her to make critical choices. Verde is a big believer in listening to the truth of her heart and her higher self. This belief is behind all her decisons and has inspired her to find significant meaning and purpose in her life. She's always been interested in spiritual wisdom, and as a young adult, she embarked on a sacred journey to India in search of God, faith, and truth. During her life, she visited many holy places around the world and sat with numerous teachers who taught her about the infinite power of choice and how we create our realities based on what we believe to be true.

Later in life, she was diagnosed with Stage 4 breast cancer. When faced with this shocking news, Verde decided to make space to listen to her intuition while looking for the best treatments available. "In the midst of so much emotional pressure, it felt as if I had lost this vital connection and I needed badly to get back to myself," she says.

After a few serendipitous events, she was led to an alternative healing center in the middle of Brazil, founded by John of God. There, she decided to take a few days to find her center again and follow their healing treatment protocol before considering following her doctor's recommmendation of a double mastectomy. It turned out to be a very tough decision at the time, as there weren't any guarantees that the treatment would be successful—plus she could be losing valuable time. Against all the odds and pressures from people close to her, Verde was eventually healed entirely and no longer needed surgery.

This was a real miracle by all accounts, and Verde now helps many people who face this terrible illness find inspiration from her unique story. She is very careful in reminding people of the value of traditional medicine yet has an important message to share on the power of listening to the voice of our hearts and higher self in the midst of challenging times.

After that, Verde went through a painful divorce. After ten years of marriage, she found herself in an abusive relationship which was killing her soul and cutting off her inner joy and happiness. Once again, she was faced with the need to make some hardcore decisions and have the courage to follow the truth that was in her heart. After her divorce was complete, Verde decided to go on a pilgrimage to Santiago de Compostela in Spain, an old medieval path that can be initiated from various parts in Europe leading to Galicia, in the northern part of the country. It was a very physically challenging journey that allowed her to quiet her busy mind that was filled with doubts and fears. Verde longed to find the stillness that only can be experienced when our minds become clear of all thoughts. She wanted to listen to her heart and to all the wisdom it had to offer regarding the next vital choices. She wanted to be able to make empowered and conscious choices that would lead her to the next few chapters in her life.

This journey was later extended to a ninety-day pilgrimage to various sacred sites of Europe, including Lourdes, Fatima, and Medjugorje, in Bosnia-Herzegovina. This experience had a powerful transformative effect on her life, helping to heal from and let go of the past entirely. Verde now produces her motivational video series called Drops of Light and is the founder and host of an interview show called Wisdom Chats; both are available on the Internet. She is a passionate communicator, life coach, and inspirational speaker who believes in sharing seeds of new consciousness and helping people feel more empowered, hopeful, and ready to live happier lives. "Even when we the face illness, life-traumatic events or death itself, we have the choice to interpret these events as opportunities to grow stronger. The right choices can crack us open to the gold within that would never be discovered if we didn't dig deeply enough. At every moment, we have the opportunity to raise our consciousness and start seeing life as an incredible journey, regardless of what happens to us," she adds.

She makes the following suggestion for deciding from the heart:

"We should always work on invoking the light inside, especially when we cannot see it around us. Through meditation and living mindfully, we can create a sacred space within ourselves to communicate with our higher self and listen to what it has to say. There are always nuggets of wisdom at each situation waiting to be revealed."

TIME TO REFLECT

———

THINKING ABOUT THIS CHAPTER, WHAT DID YOU
LEARN? WHAT CAN YOU APPLY IN YOUR LIFE?

MOTIVATE

—

WHAT MOTIVATION DO YOU FEEL STIRRING INSIDE OF YOU? WHAT'S ONE STEP YOU CAN TAKE TOWARDS NURTURING THAT FEELING OF CHANGE?

Getting out of Comfort Zone

Deep within man dwell those slumbering powers; powers that would astonish him; that he never dreamed of possessing; forces that would revolutionize his life if aroused and put into action.

—ORISON SWETT MARDEN

IT TAKES COURAGE TO GET out of your comfort zone and move ahead through the churn to achieve the success that you probably only dreamed of. Sometimes it takes time to realize the dream or even see its possibility. Even then you must keep walking through the clouds and storm, for your pot of gold is waiting on the other side of the rainbow.

The secret recipe to get out of your comfort zone to face the unknown and to overcome self-limiting beliefs was shared by Earl Nightingale, a motivational writer, and an author.

Whatever we plant in our subconscious mind and nourish with repetition and emotion will one day become a reality.

—EARL NIGHTINGALE

We all tend to live in the world the way we see, know, and are told. And we make into our belief system and our reality. We cage ourselves in a box and create walls around us even if we are suffocated to death. A pretense of being safe becomes the norm of life. But once you try venturing out of what's familiar, discomfort quickly turns into a feeling of empowerment. What I have learned and observed is that doubt kills more dreams than failure ever will. Limitations exist only if you let them; doubts exist only if you feed them; walls exist only if you build them and fear exists only if you fear them.

Another thing I have learned is to choose to be part of the population who live in the learning zone. These people are always on the lookout for what is to be discovered, what new is there to be experienced, what new can be created, and how to challenge the status quo. And this growth mindset leads to you getting out of your comfort zone and achieving dreams, attracting success.

Just about three years ago, I started a new job in UBS. Unfortunately, I was put in a group where I was not well versed with the required technology, through the group was quite promising. It proved to be over my head and led to a severe anxiety attack, where I was very close to a nervous breakdown. But then after recovering and slowly transitioning back to work, I decided to take up the challenge and focused on doing my best and overcome doubts of performing. I put myself out there to learn and execute without fear of failure. I not only prevailed, handling multiple functions and doing work spread among at least three people single-handedly but then also got a dream opportunity to work for robotic process automation in which I am now thriving and making my mark.

If you want to experience the world as it unfolds, decide to do things by being a maverick. And that is the only way to be extraordinary and have a magical experience. I have come to firmly believe that the magic of zestful living happens outside your comfort zone.

TIME TO GET INSPIRED:
Aparna Pathak: A Life Transformation Coach

Aparna Pathak is a life transformation coach. Her uniqueness lies in her ability to understand and heal people with psychosomatic problems. She is an MBA grad and a former corporate professional who left her well-established career ten years back only to live her dream. Mother Teresa has been her idol since she was ten years old. Through her work, she aspires to help people live a happy, healthy, and fulfilled life. She is an expert in yogic science and neuroscience.

Again for her too, life hasn't been a bed of roses. There have been a couple key life-changing encounters in her life. In the midst of leaving her corporate career to pursue her dream, she met with a life-threatening accident that shook her up. While still in shock and recovering from her emotional turmoil, her optimistic attitude helped her the most. She is a fighter and a believer in self. With each difficulty, she saw herself becoming stronger and confident. She has become humbler, giving, and self-believing.

She believes in her having a higher purpose and immense potential that is yet to be unleashed. Her mission is to enable people to live to their best potential. And this quest helps her to keep unlocking her inner self and keep growing. Her life mantra is "to live each day meaningfully, allowing you to make mistakes but learn quickly from them without being affected by situation or condition." Being a curious person, she feeds her curiosity with constant learning and experimenting. Like any of us, she also has her inner fears; she does not let them stop her from pursuing her dreams and inner calling.

She makes the following suggestion to live out of your comfort zone:

"Success is not achieved overnight, but it is a constantly ongoing process, and thus it is important to keep brewing and to keep overcoming fears."

TIME TO REFLECT

—

THINKING ABOUT THIS CHAPTER, WHAT DID YOU
LEARN? WHAT CAN YOU APPLY IN YOUR LIFE?

MOTIVATE

WHAT MOTIVATION DO YOU FEEL STIRRING INSIDE OF YOU? WHAT'S ONE STEP YOU CAN TAKE TOWARDS NURTURING THAT FEELING OF CHANGE?

To act with confidence and courage

Almost every successful person begins with two beliefs: The future can be better than the present and I have the power to make it so.

—David Brooks, A Journalist and Author of The Road to Character

WHY THAT IS EVEN IF we know what the right thing to do is, we end up doing what makes us look good? It is because of the urge to conform. In the process, we leave behind our true self. We seek validation of our actions in the eyes of the world outside but fail to consider that we first belong to our inside. We act according to that which meets others' criteria, be they teachers, parents, friends, sons, daughters, husbands, co-workers, and managers, Everyone other than ourselves. It prevents you from developing actions with courage, confidence, and consistency; instead, you stay satisfied in mediocrity.

It is very crucial to remember at all times that "courage is not the absence of fear; it is action in the presence of fear." Unless you can break through self-doubts and fear of failure, you cannot grow to unleash your limitless potential. You can take an example of anyone who has made it big to become successful; you will find that all of them followed their guts and vision. They acted with confidence, courage, and consistency to break the glass, resulting in them finding their magnificence. A few examples of such people who come to my mind are J. K. Rowling, Rosa Parks, Mahatma Gandhi, and Oprah Winfrey...to name some of the legends. You need to free yourself from needing to fit in to be heard or to be one of the stereotypes. You can never be yourself and be courageous if you keep looking for belongingness outside. You will then stay entangled in the world's expectations or demands. Maya Angelou shared profound and wise words for belongingness: "You are only free when you belong to no place—you belong to every place—no place at all. The price is high. The reward is great."

I overcame my struggle about belongingness and living in the eyes of others only a few years back. I never owned up to myself or saw myself as complete. At the same time, I stayed in the quest of finding my true belongingness where I could be myself, not worrying about trying to fit into some mold and yearning for seeking approval for my thoughts or actions. And because of that, the farce or the craving for belongingness outside ended one day when I accepted myself wholly and completely. I now truly belong to myself rather than to anyone else. And that was the point of emergence of my confidence, courage, and conviction. The irony is that it is always inside us, but we search outside.

Berne Brown in her book *The Gifts of Imperfection* has defined the true belongingness very vividly. "Belonging is the innate human desire to be part of something larger than us. True belonging only happens when we present our authentic, imperfect selves to the world; our sense of belonging can never be more significant than our level of self-acceptance", she writes.

TIME TO GET INSPIRED:
Linda Morrison: An enterprising woman and fitness diva

Linda Morrison is a single mom of two teenagers and a successful self-made entrepreneur. She is a fitness diva who promotes her Ageless Body brand to empower others for getting into the best shape of their lives. She attributes her being a health icon and a successful entrepreneur to digging up inside for courage, stepping up with confidence, and continuously making efforts to move forward.

When she started on her own five years back, she had no clue about using a computer or building an online presence, and yet now she has a thriving online empire. But being a health and fitness coach, she knew she had a strong passion for helping others to fulfill their dreams. She gathered the courage to start from zero by first asking for help from the people who had been successful entrepreneurs in the area of her interest, learned the different traits of creating her brand, and worked tirelessly upon her strengths to build her brand in the healthy lifestyle marketplace. While doing all these, she became overwhelmed many times, but instead of getting disheartened, she would focus on helping her clients by using her skills and strengths to build confidence for moving forward. She also never discounted self-care and followed her daily routine to develop healthy habits for eating, sleeping, and exercising. It helped her in refueling and in staying consistent in her efforts while working long hours.

She makes the following suggestion in order to unleash your limitless potential:

"The most important for each one is to know what you want from life and then courageously go ahead in achieving the dream while building confidence along the way."

TIME TO REFLECT

———

THINKING ABOUT THIS CHAPTER, WHAT DID YOU
LEARN? WHAT CAN YOU APPLY IN YOUR LIFE?

MOTIVATE

WHAT MOTIVATION DO YOU FEEL STIRRING INSIDE OF YOU? WHAT'S ONE STEP YOU CAN TAKE TOWARDS NURTURING THAT FEELING OF CHANGE?

Mindful Living

Happiness is not a goal; it is a product of life well lived.

—THEODORE ROOSEVELT

HAVE YOU EVER SEEN THE yoga cartoon of a warrior pose? The person is standing with feet wide apart; knees bent in front, arms outstretched. And six to eight squiggly bubbles are circling the head, like "What am I doing here?" "Why I am here?" "What is my life's purpose?" "Am I doing this right?" "Am I doing things right at work and home?"

The title of this cartoon is: "The Worrier Pose." And indeed, we are in this state of mind all the time while running around day in and day out. And these questions are always active in our subconscious mind as a background thread. Do we ever attend to these questions or try to go for a mental vacation in solitude to reflect upon it? No. We continue to be in this state, which prevents us from experiencing pure joy and being happy.

The most important thing in life is to be in a joyous and fulfilled state of mind. And to be in that state, you need to be fully present at the moment and attend to it with a heart filled with gratitude. And it is magically possible by three practices. These three practices are mindfulness, meaningful relationships, and gratefulness. We all have our transactional file of the daily grind, but this is about the spiritual journey. It is the path to reckon with to be in bliss 24-7 and have happiness inside and outside. These are the practices to help create and then live a life you'll love.

1. Mindfulness Meditation: Being in present and self-awareness. It is to be in the moment 100 percent.

According to Jon Kabat-Zinn, founder of the Mindfulness-Based Stress Reduction program (MBSR), mindfulness means "paying attention in a particular way, on purpose, in the present moment and non-judgmentally." In other words, when you are involved in an activity, whether it's speaking or spending time at work or with family, pay full attention. Be completely present. Dedicate your whole mind to what you are doing. Instead of thinking about yesterday or tomorrow, concentrate on what your senses tell you about that very moment and savor the experience. And it means doing things in the meditative state—where you don't go into some trance but have your mind here and now.

Let me share my experience of the practice of mindfulness meditation while running mindfully. Last November while running my fourth marathon in New York City, I was out of energy by the twentieth mile. And intuitively it dawned to me to be focused and be immersed in the beautiful running motion. I then started to feel my entire body running in synchronicity, and not lost my previous focus on tiredness and fatigue. I found myself in sync with the surroundings, feeling the gentle breeze and the cooling rains, and started using each of my senses and muscles to connect with nature, drawing energy from it. I had an extreme sense of gratitude for getting an opportunity to run this world-class race, which calmed my nerves. More importantly, I was grateful to my body for the ability to run in the marathon. And after finishing my marathon, I experienced ultimate joy and a fulfilled heart. But then I crashed.

Later, while I was recovering, I realized that my mind had taken over my body, and I had gotten into a meditative state. The experience was beyond comprehension, and for the first time, I realized that many times I had been running mindfully during my training runs with intention and attention, enjoying the moment and accepting what is. I later started reading and doing research to find a deeper understanding of how being mindful can be so meditative during running.

What I found was that doing any activity with intention, attention, being in the present moment, and acceptance is mindfulness meditation. It is being in the state of self-awareness and enjoying the experience. It is about entirely available for whatever is happening to you or to what you are involved with and being in acceptance of it to extract pure joy in day-to-day life.

2. Meaningful Relationships: Creating extraordinary connections of caring, sharing, and loving.

You must be able to create heart-based relations for being present not only physically but also mentally and emotionally. Why is this so important to be happy? Like I said earlier, happiness is about the happy state inside and outside. Mindfulness helps you in experiencing inner joy, but unless we are connecting with people and relating to them with an open heart, we cannot be happy outside. It is about reaching out, being actually available to someone in need, doing acts of kindness, caring for your fellow human being, and extending a helping hand selflessly.

What I have learned is that the only thing required to be engaged in meaningful conversation or connection is to be genuinely available at that very moment. It is about showing interest in others, to be really listening, engaging in conversation, and sharing the warmth of your presence.

Let me share examples of what it is like to be genuinely available. We all walk through doors and many times hold the door for someone. From now on, try to catch the door with the intent of helping the other person to go through, with a caring feeling and exchange a smile or eye contact. We don't realize, but it establishes a deep connection of care and compassion, which makes you feel good inside. And likewise, the positive impact on the other person and its positive vibrations are reflected on you as well. The same thing applies when you have a smile

S.O.A.R.

on your face when walking in a corridor. Another example is while driving when you allow the person to pass ahead at an intersection or raise a hand when someone lets you pass ahead. These acts of kindness are the seeds for creating joy inside and outside.

I love the saying by Maya Angelou: "Be the rainbow in someone's cloud." We are not here alone. It thus becomes even more important to be in this world building meaningful relations with our communication and interaction with others. It creates a sense of joy and happiness not only inside but also outside. It does not take a dime to be kind but goes a long way like a winding wine.

3. An attitude of gratitude: Being thankful for what you are, how you are, and where you are.

An attitude of gratitude is embracing who you are and being thankful for everything you have, had, and will be having. Unless you don't feel grateful for what you have and don't have a feeling of abundance, there is no way you can receive more from the universe and feel fulfilled.

This life is a gift from God. We came to this world with nothing, and we are here reading this book and have food to survive and a place to live. Shouldn't we be thankful for it? We are privileged souls to have all of these in this life, and we must feel grateful for it. To embrace new things in life, we need to be thankful for what we have first.

I am grateful for who I am and what I am. I am thankful every day for waking up every morning, breathing in fresh air, and be here in this beautiful world. I read somewhere this saying: "You get blues when you don't have shoes until you see someone who doesn't even have feet to wear shoes." The fact is that it is not happiness that makes us grateful; it is gratefulness that makes us happy.

He is a wise man who does not grieve for the things which
he has not, but rejoices for those which he has.

—Epictetus

49

TIME TO GET INSPIRED:

Braco Pobric: Amazon bestselling author of *Habits and Happiness*

After being an instructor for more than five years at Dale Carnegie's flagship program on leadership and improving self, Braco Pobric still wasn't sure about the one thing that makes us happy? How is success tied to happiness? That quest led him to keep researching and taking programs on the science of happiness. And he was then convinced of what happiness and success are about after learning of what Shawn Actor shared: "It is not the success that makes us happy, but it is happy people who are more successful."

According to Pobric, happiness is not found outside, but it is locked inside, which needs to be unlocked by knowing what you want to live for. "Each one of us has got a toolbox with different techniques and practices to be applied to be happier with the current condition or situation," he says. For him, mindfulness and meditation practices, nurturing positive connections and having an attitude of gratitude come on top of the tools and techniques of being happy.

He is a firm believer of morning-hour practices of exercising, meditating, and starting the day with a feeling of gratitude. It then slowly creates a positive momentum to the day in helping take life in its stride

TIME TO REFLECT

THINKING ABOUT THIS CHAPTER, WHAT DID YOU
LEARN? WHAT CAN YOU APPLY IN YOUR LIFE?

MOTIVATE

WHAT MOTIVATION DO YOU FEEL STIRRING INSIDE OF YOU? WHAT'S ONE STEP YOU CAN TAKE TOWARDS NURTURING THAT FEELING OF CHANGE?

AWAKENING 10

Stand Up, Show Up, and Speak Up

The true grit is making a decision and standing by it. Doing
what must be done. No moral man can have peace of mind if
he leaves undone what he knows he should have done.

—JOHN WAYNE

THERE IS NO BETTER EXAMPLE of the quote by Wayne than one of the dialogues between Pandava prince Arjuna and his guide and charioteer Krishna from Bhagavad Gita. It is a 700-verse Hindu scripture in Sanskrit that is part of the Hindu epic Mahabharata. Krishna asked Arjuna to stand up, show up, and roar into the battlefield of Kurukshetra for righteousness and a moral cause. When the war between Kauravas and Pandavas was on the brink of starting, the warrior Arjuna gave up his weapons, after being filled with grief and sorrow for fighting against his cousins. He succumbed to his dejection and surrendered to Lord Krishna. Lord Krishna then provided the critical knowledge in his discourse to the dejected Arjuna to enable him to get up, pick up his weapons, and come out roaring for the right cause. After attaining knowledge and wisdom, Arjuna rose to the occasion to lead the battle of Kurukshetra.

The life that we live has a constant struggle between standing up to do the right thing and avoiding falling to your crippling thoughts and negative emotions. The most important is showing up courageously and righteously while fighting the war that goes on both inside and outside of us. The inside war is what you ought to fight yourselves by raising your consciousness and growing from within.

Who you are and how you represent yourself in action displays your character. People will mirror your lead and will follow you for who you are. In this case, influence has very little to do with what you say but has everything to do with how you show up in the world, which is with conviction based on your beliefs and values.

It boils down to having a great attitude toward the challenge on hand and readiness to encounter it with a clear vision and by displaying your character strength and leadership. A great attitude makes a great day. Great days make a great month. Great months make a great year. And great years make a great life. Fulfilling success comes by standing out and not by fitting in. If you act by staging a show, your makeup will have a temporary luster; but to achieve greatness and lasting success, you must stand out being authentic, courageous, and tenacious.

I have lived most of my life behind the curtain or putting up a mask. I never showed up in the world with authenticity or being myself. It not only led to losing myself but also missing my identity over a period of time. Then a time came where I couldn't even differentiate right from wrong. My confidence level went to zero, and I faced multiple episodes of depression and self-worth went missing. And self-esteem was nowhere to be found. Later, after hitting rock bottom and having no deeper to go possibly, I picked up myself and came out, breaking my mental barriers as and preconceived notions of being weak or indecisive about taking the right steps—instead of honoring myself for who I am, what I am, and how I am. This led me to rise first in my own eyes. After regaining self-worth, I came fighting back, breaking glass walls, tearing out curtains, and smashing the mask that I had put on for years. I started to do things from my heart.

We all go through challenging times and face off with various moments of truth. Once you recognize it and embrace it with courage, you then evolve to stand out in the world for what you truly are.

TIME TO GET INSPIRED:

Yasmina Desai: A comeback woman of courage and compassion

I am very proud of my mother, Yasmina Desai for how she made her space to shine after the age of fifty-five; taking care of all her responsibilities as a daughter, wife, homemaker, and a loving mother. Her mother passed away when she was very young and was raised by her father alone. She got married at twenty-one and soon gave birth to me after a year. After four years my younger brother, Vyapak, was born, and she got immersed in taking care of both of us. Though she had a law degree, she ended up giving up her aspirations and took pride in being a homemaker and a loving and caring mother. She neither focused on her interests nor she worked upon being by her own all along and felt her belongingness to her sons, husband, and house. When the time came to move on to a new home, it created a mental upheaval due to her strong attachment and belongingness to the present house and surroundings. She also went through depression during that time. It was by mid-fifties, she took the opportunity to focus on her well-being and her interests.

She began learning yoga, and it helped her in negotiating the depressive phase that she underwent. It helped in maintaining her mental and emotional well-being. She then decided to become a yoga teacher, and it was the starting point for doing things that she liked and at the same time help others in the process. According to her, with yoga practices, she learned the principle of accepting change, being happy in any situation or condition and most importantly loving oneself. After she moved to Mumbai to live with my brother, she started showing her skills and abilities and standing up to do things of her liking along with taking care of any family or household needs. She started teaching yoga to senior citizens in the community garden daily, which she has now been doing for almost seven years. She started taking part in dance competitions. According to her, the change that was brought in her is through practices of yoga to know oneself and to go within to see things inside-out.

Presently, she is a committee member of "Mahila Parishad," an NGO for Women's rights in Mumbai, and a lead participant in the All India Women Conference for Mumbai branch.

She makes the following suggestion to overcome self-struggle:

"Whatever happens to us is always for our good, have faith in God. We realize it only afterward that a bad situation, turned out in our favor. The practice of meditation, yoga, and positive thinking helps you to keep calm and remain in a peaceful state."

TIME TO REFLECT

THINKING ABOUT THIS CHAPTER, WHAT DID YOU
LEARN? WHAT CAN YOU APPLY IN YOUR LIFE?

MOTIVATE

———

WHAT MOTIVATION DO YOU FEEL STIRRING INSIDE OF YOU? WHAT'S ONE STEP YOU CAN TAKE TOWARDS NURTURING THAT FEELING OF CHANGE?

Build Character

A character cannot be developed in ease and quiet. Only through
experience of trial and suffering the soul is strengthened,
vision cleared, ambition inspired, and success achieved.

—*HELEN KELLER*

HELEN KELLER AND HER LIFE story is a remarkable example of building a character. She was nineteen months old when she suffered from a severe illness that left her blind and deaf. Not long after, she also became mute. Her tenacious struggle to overcome these handicaps with the help of her inspiring teacher, Anne Sullivan, is one of the greatest stories of human courage and dedication.

She prevailed over seemingly insurmountable obstacles. She spoke not only for herself and others with physical disabilities but also for an array of progressive causes, including women's suffrage, pacifism, and socialism. Keller received an honorary degree from Harvard, the first ever granted to a woman that proclaimed, "From a still, dark world she has brought us light and sound; our lives are richer for her faith and her example."

"Work on building your character and not your reputation. Your character is who you are, and your reputation is what people think of who you are," said legendary coach John Wooden. Your character is the most vital of your core strengths. The stronger your character, the greater is your growth potential. The character of a person is not something you are born with; rather, it is something that is created as you overcome trials in your life. It is built over a period of time based on how you persevere through life's challenges. Ralph Waldo Emerson shared the recipe to build your character that defines your destiny. "Sow a thought, and you reap an action; sow an act, and you reap a habit; sow a habit, and you reap a character; sow a character, and you reap a destiny."

TIME TO GET INSPIRED:
Nishith Desai—The founder of Nishith Desai Associates (NDA), a leading law firm in India with offices in Singapore, Munich, and Silicon Valley

Nishith Desai is the Founder of Nishith Desai Associates (NDA), which holds the distinction of being awarded as India's Most Innovative Law Firm (2014–2017) by RSG. Even after achieving soaring success and having fame South Asia, he is a humble and down-to-earth person.

He was born in a small village in Gujarat in 1950 and was struck with the tragedy of losing his father at the age of four. He had a tough childhood full of hardships and emotional upheaval. After his mother remarried, it became unbearable for him to handle the pent-up anger and violent behavior of his stepfather. His aunt in Mumbai raised him as he refused to stay in a hostile environment at home. He was an average student while growing up with difficulty in maintaining focus, terrible in mathematics, but also a voracious reader with a curious mind. After graduating as a lawyer in 1973, he had a very slow start in his law career and struggled to make ends meet. "There have been many difficult situations in my life. What helped me the most was a steadfast belief that every problem has a solution and that one must stay super optimistic in all circumstances. That allowed me to stay focused on finding a solution to the problems rather than blaming people and circumstances around me", he says.

He prides himself on having fought for people's fundamental rights working in conjunction with Jaiprakash Narayan during the Emergency imposed by Prime Minister India Gandhi. He chose to take a courageous step to start working in High Court and be a beginner among stalwarts to expand his career and make a difference in the world of law. With money issues, his wife, Swati, supported him in his endeavors. While learning through observation in High court, he started his practice and persevered patiently doing research work and studies in the subjects of International Law and Taxation to master them. His big breakthrough came with the publication of his book on tax benefits of NRI investing in India.

From this point onward, he continued to grow globally and achieved soaring success by maintaining a focus on tax law research, keeping the client's happiness and satisfaction first, maintaining a dynamic and flexible approach in business models, and giving a distinct direction to NDA. According to him, the qualities that shaped his life and career are not compromising on ideals and ethics by any means; being quick in finding opportunities amid struggles; self-belief; adapting quickly to new situations; using his creative abilities to discover new possibilities and last but not least, never playing the victim card. Desai started with nothing but with a passion for research, fiercely determined to live life on his terms. Later, he created India's most innovative legal firm. Recently, he had an invitational meeting with India's Prime Minister Narendra Modi as well.

He makes the following suggestion to grow through challenges:

"Life is imperfect. Stay calm and in the state of "sthithpragnya" (mental balance). Look at the things objectively and interpreting it with a degree of subjectivity. And only after that, decide on the path to be taken. While one must consciously continue to remove imperfections, one must train to start the day with a mindful thought to become better than yesterday. Do everything with meditative mindset."

TIME TO REFLECT

THINKING ABOUT THIS CHAPTER, WHAT DID YOU
LEARN? WHAT CAN YOU APPLY IN YOUR LIFE?

MOTIVATE

WHAT MOTIVATION DO YOU FEEL STIRRING INSIDE OF YOU? WHAT'S ONE STEP YOU CAN TAKE TOWARDS NURTURING THAT FEELING OF CHANGE?

Have Self-Pride

You are not what others think you are; what you think, you are!

—Marcus Aurelius

IT IS VERY EASY TO get tossed around by judgments from others. You end up digging your own grave. You cave into self-pity by giving attention to it. It kills your inner voice, and you end up losing your self-esteem and self-worth. You become your own worst enemy.

Your worthiness is not determined by what the world throws at you, but by what you *make* from what's thrown at you. You can rise from the ashes or stay buried under the grave. It is up to you to decide and then act from the depth of your heart, shrugging off any negativity that you may be surrounded with to achieve greatness. The story of *Gladiator* is a classic example, where Maximus is captured to become a slave from being the commander of the army, and then is trained to be a gladiator, rising to challenge the empire. He did not judge or blame anyone but worked on himself to become something new, even against the odds. He made sure that his attitude and actions did the talking and not his mouth. It is your journey and yours to choose the path you want to take and to do what it takes to achieve greatness.

I grew up with a silver spoon in my mouth, although lacking guts and self-confidence. I had difficulty in decision-making when faced with critical situations and would get stressed out, resulting in severe anxiety. It then got aggravated, resulting in depression and subsequent anxiety attacks over time. Though I did not blame anyone or showed self-pity, I did not do anything to strengthen my core and to overcome my weaknesses.

It was only after a big jolt of being close to nervous breakdown five years ago I realized not to be driven to misery due to external factors, but I needed to control and manage my own emotions, develop mental toughness. I started working on my marathon training after I picked up running, and I started focusing on what matters— what brings me real joy and happiness. I worked on building self-efficacy and self-awareness to fight against mental weakness to do the right things with clarity and confidence. I grew out of my self-made cocoon into a strong and resilient person. I stopped judging things around me or taking in what people would say, rather became focussed on thinking and doing what I wanted to be. I realized that you cannot succeed or achieve greatness by living a pretentious life but by working on yourself and not becoming prey to people's opinions.

TIME TO GET INSPIRED:
Dr. Natalie Edmond: A licensed clinical psychologist, yoga teacher, and mindfulness meditation practitioner

Nathalie Edmond has been in clinical practice since 2003 and has worn many hats to date while providing therapy to individuals, couples, and families and group therapy to adolescents and adults. But she discovered her path to fulfilling success after going through the most challenging phase of her career. Working the last few years as an executive for a behavioral health organization affected both her personal and professional life.

There was a reorganization, and she found herself doing multiple roles for several years, which was very emotionally draining. There was a lot of anxiety in the organization, and she was in a new position with a lot of responsibilities but also a lot of ambiguity in many ways, which meant expectations for her role were continually changing. She felt isolated as she did not have many of peers. She also had two young children at that time. She found herself emotionally distraught on most days, and the professional goals she had always thought were essential to her started to be challenged.

There was a two-year period where all of this was unfolding—from 2013 to 2015, where her daily meditation practice was extremely helpful in helping her gain clarity about her values and what was now vital to her. She found herself able to sort through her various feelings about the challenging interpersonal dynamics playing out at work. She also went through a two-hundred-hour yoga teacher training at that time, which helped her to learn to use movement as a form of meditation. She was able to learn to have compassion for people whom she perceived as making her daily work life nearly unbearable. She ultimately decided to leave the hospital where she had worked for twelve years. She chose to prioritize self-care, working in a less stressful environment and being her boss. She decided to ride the wave of fear and the unknown and start over again, which was the key to liberation.

She thinks that self-reflection and understanding the mind-body-spirit connection help to discern the different parts of us. She believes that some people can do this type of inner work on their own, while others need a therapist or some other kind of coach to help them work through trauma and other barriers to true self-love. She also suggests that there are teachers everywhere. Every interaction with another being is a possibility to learn about ourselves.

She is a big believer in developing mindfulness skills that allow you to start being an observer of your experience. With practice, you start noticing that you are not your thoughts, judgments, or feelings. It can also help you be more in the flow and the balance being in the doing mode. The main issue of many people is to commit to sitting since they don't know how to be still or be in the moment. She helps with meditation practices that focus on developing joy, gratitude, wonder, and loving kindness.

She makes the following suggestion to avoid owning up to any judgments:

"We have a brain that has a negativity bias and tends to compare and judge, but we can learn skills not to allow decisions to be made in a reactively based on judgments."

TIME TO REFLECT

———

THINKING ABOUT THIS CHAPTER, WHAT DID YOU LEARN? WHAT CAN YOU APPLY IN YOUR LIFE?

MOTIVATE

WHAT MOTIVATION DO YOU FEEL STIRRING INSIDE OF YOU? WHAT'S ONE STEP YOU CAN TAKE TOWARDS NURTURING THAT FEELING OF CHANGE?

Build Self-Esteem

You are the master of your own ship, pal. There are lots of people who
fall into troubled waters and don't have the guts or the knowledge or the
ability to make it to shore. They have nobody to blame but themselves.

—EVEL KNIEVEL

WHAT MATTERS THE MOST IS what you see when you look at yourself in
the mirror. It is not about judging yourself or allowing others to judge
you, nor is it about blaming yourself or taking the blame from others.
It is vital to know yourself, accept yourself, love yourself, and thus help
yourself to overcome insecurities. The self-esteem gets destroyed if you
see yourself less or inferior.

The most influential factor for success is self-esteem. Believing you
can do something, you deserve it, and you will get it is all necessary com-
ponents. A combination of self-confidence, self-efficacy, and self-mastery forms a key to self-esteem. The first part is to act regardless of how
you are feeling or what situation you are in or if you are being judged. It
builds self-confidence. The second part is to develop the ability to listen
to your inner voice and take action based on it. It leads to developing
self-efficacy. And finally, you must acknowledge your self-worth, which
builds self-esteem.

None of us are strong or weak. We all may have different qualities
and skills, but that does not define who you are. What defines you is how

you see yourself inside and what you project yourself outside. It is about living inside out. You need to build strong values, follow self-discipline, and have self-worth to march like a lion and be a lion.

I learned three golden rules the hard way. Firstly, if you don't respect yourself, no one else will. Secondly, if you don't treat yourself well, no one else will. Thirdly, if you don't take pride and honor in yourself, no one else will. What matters is your self-esteem and not how others see you, judge you, or treat you. It all boils down to having self-esteem. And since I lacked it, I suffered through my anxiety and depression because I saw myself as weak, timid, and complacent while handling the challenges in front of me. I depended on outside help and support to navigate through situations or issues that I faced rather than developing self-mastery.

I finally learned and realized that you hold the steering of your ship, and the more you work on yourself, the more you are in control of your ship.

TIME TO GET INSPIRED:
Ary Santos: Challenged the status quo and saw himself as a winner to become one!

Ary Santos lived a tough life while growing up, facing myriad adversities. He was born on an island called São Luis, Maranhão, in Brazil, and had a humble and impoverished childhood. His mother was his only support system since his father was not around. He grew up and studied in the small town, and then at the age of fourteen, he moved to his uncle's house in the city of São Lous where he continued advancing in his studies. He completed high school after moving to the city of Monte Dorado where his uncle and brother lived. He went through some tough without a job since he had to move back to Sao Luis, and he then shifted to Sao Paulo in 1999 in search of a good job.

After much struggle and with the help of his cousins, he finally landed a job as a stockbroker. He started in the corporate world from the bottom and worked hard to move his way up. He kept working on himself by learning new skills and embraced an opportunity, when it arose, to work in the area of technology. He accepted the challenge and kept investing time in studies to learn things in technology while overcoming different obstacles and negotiating insecurities of living alone. He says, "When we get an opportunity to learn and grow to be in any situation, we must hold and hug it because we will not always have or get another such opportunity." He indeed accepted whatever situations and circumstances he had to go through without judging or blaming anyone for it. He kept his focus on building self-confidence, self-efficacy, and self-worth along the way without having self-pity.

He was hit by another blow when he was diagnosed with a medical condition, in which he had to lose at least 10 kg in a year. He again rolled up his sleeves and took on the challenge. He made a conscious decision to do whatever it took to get his weight under control. He started with physical activities at the gym, but the process of weight reduction was slow. He then researched various options to slim down faster and joined the group "A Year of Running." In the beginning, he started to run alone, which became a habit, and kept increasing the distance little by little. Within three months, he had already run a twenty-km race; in five months, he ran his first thirty-km race, and in seven months, he ran his first marathon. He got his weight under 75 kg, well below of what was required for his well-being.

He attributes his accomplishment to his attitude of taking on challenges without caving into self-pity. He kept focus and stayed disciplined toward his goal. He continues to run marathons, which has now become a part of his life.

He makes the following suggestion to work towards self-worth:

"Setting goals and objectives and having determination is the key because the strength of will and courage take us where we want. Never miss an opportunity to develop by working on yourself by staying determined to be worthy of something."

TIME TO REFLECT

THINKING ABOUT THIS CHAPTER, WHAT DID YOU
LEARN? WHAT CAN YOU APPLY IN YOUR LIFE?

MOTIVATE

WHAT MOTIVATION DO YOU FEEL STIRRING INSIDE OF YOU? WHAT'S ONE STEP YOU CAN TAKE TOWARDS NURTURING THAT FEELING OF CHANGE?

Work on Self-Control

Do your thing. Do it unapologetically. Don't be discouraged by criticism.
You probably know what they are going to say. Pay no mind to fear
of failure. It is far more valuable than success. Take ownership, take
chances and have fun. And no matter what never stop doing your thing.

—UNKNOWN

IF YOU WANT TO STAY ordinary, that is your choice. But if you want to achieve greatness and be a high achiever, there is no other way then being disciplined and work upon what is to be done to realize your fullest potential. Staying focused on your goals, canceling outside noise, and staying committed to going ahead with full throttle is the way to accomplish your goal.

Self-control makes you more focused on what truly matters to do what must be done to achieve your goal. It helps to stay away from things that do not serve you or your purpose or the mission. It broadens your willpower and increases your ability to leap into the unknown, breaking the barriers of mind cuffs and limiting beliefs. Jim Rohn says, which is so apt, "The formula for success is a few simple disciplines practiced every day." Like a muscle, the more you apply self-control, the stronger you get. As your self-control increases, you gain the ability to direct your life in a manner that is congruent with the true you. Self-control is nothing but controlling your mind or self-discipline. The more disciplined you are, the better you can be; just like mind over matter. I like the way actor Will Smith puts it, saying, "There's a redemptive power that making a choice has. Decide what you're going to be, who you are going to be, and then how you are going out into a place to make it happen for you."

On doing some retrospection, it took the daily discipline of going out to run no matter what and having the self-control to overcome the mind chatter of "ifs" and "buts" of excuses to forge my way ahead to become a "MarathonForLife" runner, which is my alter ego. It was not easy to go out for a run early morning every day, but I now realize that I needed to have self-control and do what was to be done to break out from doubt, fear, and self-imposed limitation. That choice fueled me with energy, building up confidence and leading me to freedom in overcoming mental barriers and blocks.

TIME TO GET INSPIRED:
Wayne Gills: Keynote Speaker, Author, and Traumatic Brain Injury Survivor!

Wayne Gills is a former employee trainer in a prestigious bank, father of two little sons, and a loving husband sold a successful business in Florida before returning to Canada to go back to university to pursue a career in medicine. In 2005, however, a car struck his motorcycle; apart from all other damage, a traumatic brain injury momentarily shattered his life. Among his numerous physical injuries were seven broken ribs, a ruptured spleen, a bruised liver, a torn bowel, and a bilateral pneumothorax (two punctured lungs).

After going through critical brain surgery and staying unconscious for four weeks, his vital signs improved to give indications of him waking up. And he finally gained consciousness on the fourth day earlier than what was expected, which was his rebirth to script his story of hope, recovery, and determination. He was given a second chance on life.

It took a total of seven years for his full recovery against all possible odds, which in a way itself is a miracle. His consistent hope and determination to achieve the desired outcome helped him to maintain a positive outlook toward his improvement. Based on his journey and the number of challenges he overcame, he says, "You have to be motivated to do something and inspired to pursue that direction, but ultimately, achieving a goal comes down to the individual's choice to do it. No matter how motivated you are, how inspired you have become, you must be personally determined to succeed." His approach is adapting to what is delivered your way. You're no longer reacting; rather, you are proactively redirecting your focus to attain the desired outcome. And this requires a tremendously disciplined mind and the self-control to put aside all negativity, especially when you are rising from both cognitive and physiological impaired conditions.

He shares his living philosophy in his book *Moving Forward*. In it, he vows to live life on a daily basis, and not let life live him. Following is the mantra he adopted to maintain a constant positive outlook— overcoming the emotional upheaval with hope and determination.

"When you change your expectations, you change your attitude. When you change your attitude, you change your behavior. When you change your behavior, you change your performance. When you change your performance, you change your life!"

TIME TO REFLECT

—

THINKING ABOUT THIS CHAPTER, WHAT DID YOU
LEARN? WHAT CAN YOU APPLY IN YOUR LIFE?

MOTIVATE

WHAT MOTIVATION DO YOU FEEL STIRRING INSIDE OF YOU? WHAT'S ONE STEP YOU CAN TAKE TOWARDS NURTURING THAT FEELING OF CHANGE?

Gain Self-Mastery

*Self-mastery is a challenge for every individual. Only we can
control our own appetite and passions. Self-mastery cannot
be bought by money or get through fame. It is the ultimate
test of our character. It requires climbing out of deep valleys
of our lives and scaling our own Mount Everest.*

—JAMES E. FAUST

SELF-MASTERY IS GAINED THROUGH HAVING self-awareness, self-discipline,
self-control, and self-compassion. Mastery over a skill can be attained
through practice, deliberate focus, and continuous self-improvement, while
self-mastery is about living up to the highest calling and virtues. You no
longer need to force yourself to do something to achieve a goal. You keep
pursuing excellence in your endeavors on a daily basis—becoming better
each day then becomes your way of life.

It happens from having patience, truthfulness, purity, impeccabil-
ity, and faith. It requires patience to accept what already is and the wisdom to know when to allow things to unfold in their own time. In other
words, you need to be true not only in your words and actions but also,
to be honest with yourself. You need to be pure in your lifestyle through
a healthy diet, regular exercise, and adequate sleep. You need to be the
best you can in all you do, with humility and respect. You need to have

faith in the path you have chosen, trust in your teachers, and confidence in your ability to be masterful. Maharishi Mahesh Yogi, a spiritual leader from India; used to say, "Capture the fort and all the territory will be yours." There are many examples of those who attained self-mastery over a period of time. Some names that come to mind include Mozart, Picasso, Steve Jobs, Lois Armstrong, and Michael Phelps, people who attained self-mastery with their dedication, commitment, and disciplined efforts.

For me, self-mastery is the journey, and I continuously keep working on myself to be my best possible self along the way. With self-awareness and focus on self-improvement, I am now a 5:00 a.m. person, and I do running/workout daily, eat only healthy veggies for my lunch, maintain a gratitude journal, perform acts of kindness, do systematic giving to charity, and continue developing a growth mindset from a fixed mindset. And I believe in my quote to accept, embrace, and evolve to achieve greatness.

TIME TO GET INSPIRED:

Michael Albert: A nationally acclaimed collage artist

Born and brought up in New York, Albert is living a happy married life with four children in New Jersey. He graduated as a business major. Along with co-founding a food distribution marketing company, Albert created his brand, the Sir Real Juice Company. He developed an interest in drawing and writing poems. He continues doing it, and now he is a well-known collage artist and recently published An Artist of America. He has sold/distributed over 10,000 posters so far and conducted his workshops at over 1000 venues.

Though now being successful in many areas, the journey wasn't easy for him either. While he was developing his talent and mastering it, he stayed patient, humble, and confident

He believes that you need strong convictions about what you are trying to achieve. Knowing you may never reach it in this life, you should be resigned to the fact that the journey is as important (in fact more important than) the goal itself. The journey is made up of many steps to get to where you're going, and each level is significant and critical. He says, "If you continue to work toward your goals, step by step, day by day on what interests you that makes you happy, productive, and worthwhile, which will then evolve into passion and result into growth and satisfaction." He strongly calls for practicing humility while doing whatever you do to help achieve your goals.

He makes the following these suggestions to achieve fulfilling success:

"Be grateful for what you have or had, be flexible to roll sustaining punches on the face, and be ready to deal with unsuspected things and challenges without getting disheartened; keep a strong faith in the higher power."

TIME TO REFLECT

———

THINKING ABOUT THIS CHAPTER, WHAT DID YOU LEARN? WHAT CAN YOU APPLY IN YOUR LIFE?

MOTIVATE

—

WHAT MOTIVATION DO YOU FEEL STIRRING INSIDE OF
YOU? WHAT'S ONE STEP YOU CAN TAKE TOWARDS
NURTURING THAT FEELING OF CHANGE?

Generate Self-Drive

"Capacity, Audacity and Tenacity will take you to your mountaintop."

—ROBIN SHARMA

LIVING WITH AUDACITY AND TENACITY while fighting your fears is the best bet you can ever make with your life. With that, even if you fail; you succeed. You learn from your fall to rise to a new challenge. You realize your true potential when you keep moving forward. It is crucial to keep taking courageous actions aligned with your vision, purpose, and values because if you don't, you are moving backward since the world is still moving ahead.

Richard Branson says, "You don't learn to walk by following rules. You learn by doing, and by falling over." I learned about converting disadvantage to advantage and its significance from Branson. He is one of my idols because of his entrepreneurial spirit when it comes to courage and following your instincts. Diagnosed with dyslexia, Branson left school at the age of sixteen because he was unable to follow the curriculum. But he turned the disadvantage into an advantage as an entrepreneur.

While reviewing Virgin's advertising and marketing, Branson's colleagues read everything aloud, giving him a sense of the overall concept and allowing him to weed out industry jargon in favor of ordinary language. When Branson did the launch of Virgin Atlantic airlines in 1984 and Virgin Australia in 2000, his fellow board members were skeptical about the chances for success. But Branson recognized an opportunity and stuck to it—and it has paid off. Virgin Atlantic now carries more than five million passengers a year, and Virgin Australia has become the country's second-largest airline. "Whenever something goes wrong, or you find yourself at a disadvantage, often the best way to handle it is to turn a negative into a positive," Branson says.

TIME TO GET INSPIRED

Sandy Joy Weston: An instructor, a trainer, an entrepreneur, a health club owner, and a media personality

Weston is a high-energy and vibrant person on both the physical and spiritual levels, which has helped her attain to new heights of being. At the same time, she has gone through tough times while growing up. Weston ended up living in a public housing project, and, with her mother in and out of mental institutions, it made her life very unpredictable. But deep down she always had the faith to keep on going and not succumbing to unfavorable circumstances. She persevered through all her hardships and struggles, focusing on her passion for dance and a compulsion to make something of her talents and aspirations.

At a very early age, she learned to be bold in thinking, have courageous actions, and be tenacious in her approach to accomplishing goals. Under all kind of adversity, she managed to stick to her goals, attending undergraduate studies in the school of her choice on a scholarship based on her dance, and eventually going on to study for M.Ed.

She quickly became the most sought-after coach for the fitness management of women at the high end of the market. According to her, "What made these ladies attracted to me and to support me without judgment was due to my authenticity and courageousness in what I do or say." It led her to launch herself as a fitness trainer during times when it was not a leading profession, especially among women. She went on to open a state-of-the-art facility in the heart of Philadelphia called

"Weston Fitness," which is now flourishing and growing due to her positive attitude, zeal, and vigor.

She firmly believes that the only way to succeed against all the odds is to give your best and act courageously with faith and determination. She recently published her book titled Train Your Head and Your Body Will Follow: Reach Any of Your Fitness Goals in 3 Minutes a Day.

She makes the following suggestion to generate self-drive:

"Never let people shape your future; rather follow your passion, make the resolve, and unless it is properly cooked in your head don't disclose it to outside world to prevent being crippled down."

TIME TO REFLECT

———

THINKING ABOUT THIS CHAPTER, WHAT DID YOU
LEARN? WHAT CAN YOU APPLY IN YOUR LIFE?

MOTIVATE

WHAT MOTIVATION DO YOU FEEL STIRRING INSIDE OF YOU? WHAT'S ONE STEP YOU CAN TAKE TOWARDS NURTURING THAT FEELING OF CHANGE?

Be Optimistic

"Don't cry because it's over, smile because it happened."

—DR. SEUSS

OPTIMISM IS SEEING THE POSITIVE side of every equation. It is turning a bad situation into your favor with your positive attitude and outlook. Why is being optimistic essential to do what you want and to be what you want? Because being optimistic is the single and most important ingredient out of all others to help a person to keep moving forward. If you slide into becoming a pessimist, you kill your growth by creating a dam to block your flow of thoughts, energy, creativity, and liveliness.

You have to be optimistic about everything you engage in, everything you undertake on this life's journey. Unless you maintain a positive stance in your approach, receiving a positive outcome with the help from the universe is not only difficult but also gets to the point that it becomes impossible. This world is full of possibilities and abundance of all things that could be available to you. You have to synchronize your optimism with a positive outlook to open channels for tapping into it while staying grateful every step along the way. Not every event turns into your advantage or meets your highest expectations. Still, as long as you are an optimist, it will help you to appreciate things as they happen and to keep moving forward. The setback is just a learning experience and becomes an opportunity to improve upon your efforts to go ahead with an even better plan and directed action

Steve Jobs always said, "You can't connect the dots looking forward; you can only connect them looking backward. So you have to trust that the dots will somehow connect in your future and keep moving forward. You have to trust in something—your gut, destiny, life, karma, whatever." Isn't that profound? If you read his biography by Walter Isaacson, you will realize that without his optimism there was no way he would have gone ahead to build his legacy, revolutionizing digital, phone, tablet, movie, and music industries with a mix of his roller-coaster life and the searingly intense personality of a creative entrepreneur.

My personal life also resonates with his to a certain extent, having gone through a roller-coaster ride of life. My firm belief in myself that there is something special inside me to be unleashed and bring forth in this world has been my only ray of hope. I did not know when and how. With that faith and by remaining patient while facing various jolts of anxiety and depression, I kept moving forward and grew from within each time to end up rediscovering my true passion, purpose, and potential. Keeping that positive mindset is not easy when you encounter terrible blows chronically and undergo close to a nervous breakdown. But then that is how you learn life's toughest lessons. The reason to be optimistic in even dire conditions is that there is a silver lining in every cloud that you have to believe in and learn to see. When you genuinely believe in yourself and keep an optimistic approach, the universe comes to your rescue and eventually guides you to your ultimate destiny.

TIME TO GET INSPIRED:

Sapan Shah: An optimist all the way

Sapan is an excellent friend of mine, whom I met for the first time about eighteen years ago. He came from a middle-class family back in India and was raised very frugally. His upbringing laid the foundation to not depend on parents or anyone but instead to make something of him. He learned at a very early age during college that a person needs to strive on their own to achieve their goal or to fulfill their wishes and desires. He was not a topper in his class nor did he have an exceptionally high IQ, but he undoubtedly possessed an extraordinarily strong will and high aspirations. He came to the US, to the land of opportunity, twenty years ago after his marriage. He presently sees himself accomplished, happy, and content, having a wife, twin beautiful teen daughters, and a job at a high corporate position in the financial sector in a reputed bank. But his journey hasn't been a cakewalk.

After coming to the US, he faced some severe challenges both personally and professionally. One of the most significant problems was the language barrier since he had studied until college in Gujarati, the local language where he grew up, and could hardly speak English. To break the wall, he started watching news channels and reading newspapers as much as he could while keeping a dictionary with him all the time. At the same time, he began working as a cashier at a local convenience store, which helped him in speaking/communicating with people. He still remembers the broken English that he talked at that time, but he overcame that problem by his ardent desire to make himself better. He continued keeping the positive outlook. Another challenge was to develop a personality for competing in the corporate world and culture. He worked on transforming himself to not only blend in his adopted society but also distinguish himself in the community. According to him, "Your personality and how you carry yourself speaks of you since that's the first thing people look at, so it better be good." His sincere effort and determination paid off, and being a quick learner; he was able to make strides in his personal development, which culminated in him obtaining a good position in the bank where he quickly climbed to the rank of senior vice president. He continues to improve his vocabulary to become a better communicator and excel in his role professionally.

He firmly believes in visualizing the person you want to be. "Self-improvement is the key to unlock your hidden potential. Continuous learning and growing are vital to gather knowledge, skills, and abilities," he says. He focused on knowing his strengths and weaknesses to improve his core competencies and succeed in the professional world. The most important takeaway from his fulfilling success is to create your brand, to surround yourself with like-minded people, to develop an exciting personality, and to be open-minded. His optimism in handling life's challenges was fueled by continually keeping the picture of what he wants to be in life in front of his mind's eye. He always wanted to be part of something bigger than routine life, where he could make a difference in his society or community with his skills and knowledge to live a meaningful life.

He makes the following suggestion to live powerfully:

"Find your passion. Be brutally honest when doing introspection. And learn to say 'no' for things that don't align with what matters most to you."

TIME TO REFLECT

THINKING ABOUT THIS CHAPTER, WHAT DID YOU
LEARN? WHAT CAN YOU APPLY IN YOUR LIFE?

MOTIVATE

WHAT MOTIVATION DO YOU FEEL STIRRING INSIDE OF
YOU? WHAT'S ONE STEP YOU CAN TAKE TOWARDS
NURTURING THAT FEELING OF CHANGE?

Be Gritty

*To be gritty is to keep putting one foot in front of the other. To be gritty
is to hold fast to an interesting and purposeful goal. To be gritty
is to invest, day after week after year, in challenging the practice.
To be gritty is to fall down seven times, and rise the eighth time!*

—ANGELA DUCKWORTH, MACARTHUR *"GENIUS"*
GRANTS WINNER, RESEARCHER, AND AUTHOR OF GRIT:
THE POWER OF PASSION AND PERSEVERANCE

GRIT IS SOMETHING YOU CAN build and develop whether you have the
talent or not. Yes, it may take more time to attain self-mastery, but as
long as it interests you and if you are ready to devote 100 percent for
an extended period to harness your skill, growth and fulfilling success
is definite. We all have talents, and many times we tap into it, resulting
in positive experience and outcome. But unless we harness that talent,
develop it into a passion, and persevere while building it, it withers out
with time.

Why do I consider grit as the final frontier for growing from within
and unleashing your limitless potential? Grit involves all the key ele-
ments that are required for success and fulfillment. First and foremost,
you need a resolution and discipline for pursuing a goal for the long
term, using the talent you have or in an area of your interest to build

your skill. Mostly you gravitate to your innate talent since it provides you the natural impetus to make it your life's focus. It then requires courage to stand the test of time and self-control to persevere and be consistent in your efforts no matter how long it may take to obtain what you're seeking.

After reading Duckworth's latest book *GRIT: The Power of Passion and Perseverance* and following all her research around these concepts, I have come to believe that grit is the measure of you becoming what you want to be. It is the final frontier because, in the end, everything comes down to the power of passion and perseverance that truly unleashes your limitless potential. Research suggests that your talent either stays at the baseline or even goes below in comparison to others if you don't apply and practice for an extended period. In order words to build self-mastery, utilize your fullest potential, and for achieving fulfilling success, you need to make your life's long-term goal to master your talent and skills purposefully.

There is no better example that I can think of other than Will Smith. Smith has a track record of success that anybody would envy. He's one of the few artists to have enjoyed great success in three different entertainment fields: TV, music, and movies. In the 1980s, he started as a rapper under the name The Fresh Prince with modest success, but he quickly rose to fame after taking the title role in the TV series The Fresh Prince of Bel-Air. After the series ended, Smith moved to star in movies. He has starred in several Hollywood blockbusters like Men In Black, iRobot, The Pursuit of Happiness, Ali, and Bad Boys. Smith is the only actor to have eight consecutive movies to earn more than $100 million at the worldwide box office. Through his films, his love for life, and his speeches, he has become an inspiration to millions of people around the world. When asked the core reason and key to his success as compared to many of his peers, Smith points out, "The separation of talent and skill is one of the greatest misunderstood concepts for people who are trying to excel, who have dreams, who want to do things. Talent you have naturally. Skill is only developed by hours and hours and hours of beating on your craft. I never viewed myself as particularly talented. Where I excel is ridiculous, sickening, work ethic. You know, while the other guy's sleeping, I'm working." And finally, he goes out to say, "If you challenge me to be on the treadmill, the only outcome of running in it is that either the other person loses or I die.", which is the core of having grit.

I feel that it is grit that led me to the point where running is now a part of my life. There have been no consecutive days without me not having gone for a run. And it has undoubtedly changed my life and being. My passion is now to continue to unleash my limitless potential, and I aspire to bring my vigor, zest, and vitality into everything I do. The urge to overcome self-limiting beliefs and eagerness to find more wholesome possibilities led me to achieve one of the greatest feats of my life. I climbed Mount Kilimanjaro in September 2018. Mount Kilimanjaro is the world's highest free-standing mountain, and, at 19,341 feet, it is one of seventh highest summits in the world.

TIME TO GET INSPIRED:
Dr. Caren Baruch-Feldman: Psychologist, Marathon Runner, and Author of the Grit Guide for Teens

When I asked Baruch-Feldman what the most challenging thing that she had faced so far was, she recalled her first experience of being confronted with the mammoth task of an honors thesis in college. She had the choice to give up and complete it with a regular thesis. But she dug deep to muster up the spirit to move forward, reached out to people having expertise in the subject, put in the necessary time to get a grasp of the topic that she liked instead of worrying about the effort needed, and took up the challenge to go with an honors thesis. It was not the thesis she completed that she is most proud of but how she ignited her passion and persevered, focusing on all the resources on hand, which built her into a strong, resilient person.

After her Ph.D. in psychology, she started blogging on the topics of wellness, growth, applying your strengths and resilience specifically for teens. And she went ahead and wrote a book specifically to help build perseverance, self-control, and a growth mindset for teens titled The Grit Guide for Teens: A Workbook to Help You Build Perseverance, Self-Control, and a Growth Mindset.

She continues to build upon her key to success in every part of life. She went on to run the New York Marathon and also a 50-mile bike race across all the five boroughs of New York. She believes in inspiring a growth mindset. For any of us to accomplish real change we need persistence, grit, and a positive outlook. Helping people to achieve this "yes" mindset to create a positive change is her goal. She acknowledges that being gritty and having self-control in the face of temptations and rebounding from failures not easy.

She shares these ten strategies for growing your grit from her blog The Secret Recipe for GRIT published in Huffington Post:

1. FRAME BEHAVIOR IN THE POSITIVE—Highlight positive aspects rather than focusing on the deprivation.
2. MAKE IT EASY TO BE GRITTY AND HARD TO GIVE IN TO TEMPTATION—Create the conditions to avoid getting derailed.
3. BE SPECIFIC AND DON'T TAKE ON TOO MUCH ALL AT ONCE—It's easier to tackle big problems if you take it on in small, manageable steps.
4. WRITE IT DOWN AND MONITOR YOURSELF—Make goals actionable by scripting the essential moves and be specific.
5. PRE-COMMIT TO ACTION—Pre-committing makes it difficult to reverse your preferences.
6. MAKE IT PUBLIC AND GET SOCIAL SUPPORT—By letting people know what you are doing, you pre-commit and as a result, have a better chance of changing your ways. In addition, when

you are faced with a challenge, you can access that needed social support to get you right back in the game.

7. STAND FIRM, NO WAVERING—It is to help you persist by telling yourself there is "no choice, this is what I am doing!"

8. CHANGE YOUR ENVIRONMENT AND AVOID YOUR TRIGGERS—Triggers will block you at every turn.

9. DEVELOP BELIEFS THAT WILL INSPIRE YOU—Focus on long-term goals as opposed to immediate gratification. Having a growth mindset and being passionate about your future inspires grittier behavior.

10. GET BACK ON TRACK AND DON'T OVERREACT WHEN YOU MESS UP—Learn from a lapse in the action plan instead of overreacting and causing way more damage.

TIME TO REFLECT

THINKING ABOUT THIS CHAPTER, WHAT DID YOU
LEARN? WHAT CAN YOU APPLY IN YOUR LIFE?

MOTIVATE

WHAT MOTIVATION DO YOU FEEL STIRRING INSIDE OF YOU? WHAT'S ONE STEP YOU CAN TAKE TOWARDS NURTURING THAT FEELING OF CHANGE?

Conclusion

This poem by Christian D. Larson summarizes the eighteen awakenings that I have shared. They are now part of who I am.

"Promise Yourself

To be so strong that nothing can disturb your peace of mind.

To talk health, happiness, and prosperity to every person you meet.

To make all your friends feel that there is something in them.

To look at the sunny side of everything and make your optimism come true.

To think only the best, to work only for the best, and to expect only the best.

To be just as enthusiastic about the success of others as you are about your own.

To forget the mistakes of the past and press on to the greater achievements of the future.

To wear a cheerful countenance at all times and give every living creature you meet a smile.

To give so much time to the improvement of yourself that you have no time to criticize others.

To be too large for worry, too noble for anger, too strong for fear, and too happy to permit the presence of trouble.

To think well of yourself and to proclaim this fact to the world, not in loud words but great deeds.

To live in faith that the whole world is on your side so long as you are true to the best that is in you."

—*Christian D. Larson, Your Forces and How to Use Them*

Living the virtues shared through my eighteen awakenings will surely help you in becoming the person that you want to be. The most important aspect is to have self-belief, to adopt a growth mindset, and to have a positive attitude toward life.

Let the insights gained from each nugget of knowledge from my awakenings in the book ignite your passion after reflecting upon them to grow from within and to unleash your limitless potential.

The first nugget of knowledge: *Find Your Passion and Purpose to Reach Your Full Potential!*

The second nugget of knowledge: *Once Your Why Is Clear, the How Part Becomes Easy!*

The third nugget of knowledge: *Your Idols and Values Are the Guiding Torch!*

The forth nugget of knowledge: *Kindness Is Not an Act; It Is a Lifestyle!*

The fifth nugget of knowledge: *Be Patient, and Persevere through the Process with Consistency!*

The sixth nugget of knowledge: *Make a Choice to Take a Chance for a Massive Change!*

The seventh nugget of knowledge: *Magic Happens Outside the Comfort Zone!*

The eight nugget of knowledge: *Act with Confidence, Courage, and Consistency!*

The night nugget of knowledge: *Mindfulness, Meaningful Relationships, and Attitude of Gratitude Are the Pillars of Sustained Happiness!*

The tenth nugget of knowledge: *Stand Up, Show Up, and Speak Up to Stand Out!*

The eleventh of knowledge: *Your character is destiny!*

The twelfth nugget of knowledge: *Stop Judging, and Stop Owning Judgments!*

The thirteenth nugget of knowledge: *What You See, You Become!*

The fourteenth nugget of knowledge: *Attain Self-Control for Freedom from Mind Cuffs!*

The fifteenth nugget of knowledge: *Attain Self-Mastery with Disciplined Efforts!*

The sixteenth nugget of Knowledge: *Develop Self-drive with Audacity and Tenacity!*

The seventeenth nugget of knowledge: *When You Convert Expectation into Appreciation, Life Becomes a Celebration!*

The eighteenth nugget of knowledge: *To have Grit is the Final Frontier!*

In the end, it boils down to putting what we learn into action. When knowledge is infused with action, and by living it, you will be on the path of growth and reaching your full potential. I strongly urge you to apply your take away motivation from each of the chapters in your daily life to take charge of yourself and to **S.O.A.R.** - that is, to Stand Out, be Outstanding, be Approachable, and be Remarkable in life.

References of the
Featured Inspirations:

Chapter	Title	Feature Inspiration
Awakening 1	Passion and Purpose	**Sparsh Shah** Singer/Songwriter/Rapper/ Inspirational Speaker—Inspiring billions to find their passion in life and live life to the fullest. Social Media: www.youtube.com/c/sparshpurhythm, www.facebook.com/purhythm
Awakening 2	What is your Why?	**Mel Robbins** Bestselling Author of *The 5 Second Rule: Transform your Life, Work, and Confidence with Everyday Courage*, Entrepreneur and contributing editor to *SUCCESS* Magazine Social Media: www.melrobbins.com
Awakening 3	What are your idols and values?	**Tawanda Gladman** Entrepreneur, Hair Stylist
Awakening 4	Be Kind	**Nadya Zilov** Leader, Coach, Mindfulness Practitioner

Awakening 5	Be Patient And Persevere	**Christopher Connors** Author of *The Value of You: The Guide to Living Boldly and Joyfully Through the Power of Core Values* Coach and Business Consultant Email: christdconnors@gmail.com
Awakening 6	Decision to Change	**Susie Verde** Founder of the Joy of Being Network, Certified Transformational Life Coach—An agent of joy and transformation through the power of love. Social Media: www.susieverde.com
Awakening 7	Getting out of Comfort Zone	**Aparna Pathak** Life Transformation Coach: Emotion, Mind, and Body
Awakening 8	To act with confidence and courage	**Linda Morrison** Body and Life Business Coach Ambassador of health and confidence for women of forty and over Social Media: www.lindamorrison.au
Awakening 9	Mindful Living	**Braco Pobric** Amazon bestselling author of *Habits and Happiness* A founding member and Chief Happiness Officer of the Institute for Advanced Human Performance Leader and Happiness Expert Social Media: www.habitsandhappiness.com
Awakening 10	Stand Up, Show Up, and Speak Up	**Yasmina Desai** Mother, homemaker, caregiver, yoga teacher, dancer
Awakening 11	Build Character	**Nishith Desai** Founder of Nishith Desai Associates (NDA), the most innovative Indian legal firm Social Media www.nishithdesai.com

Awakening 12	Have Self-Pride	**Dr. Nathalie Edmond** Clinical Psychologist, Yoga Teacher, and Mindfulness Meditation Practitioner Social Media: www. Drnatemond.com
Awakening 13	Build Self-Esteem	**Ary Santos** Entrepreneur, Marathon Runner
Awakening 14	Work on Self-Control	**Wayne Gills, CDNSP** Keynote Speaker and Author—Take care of your body. It's the only place you have to live! Social Media: www.always-adapt.com
Awakening 15	Gain Self-Mastery	**Michael Albert** Cereal Box Collage Pop Artist and Sir Real Juice Company Founder & Owner Social Media: www.michaelalbert.com
Awakening 16	Generate Self-Drive	**Sandy Joy Weston** Fitness Guru, Author, and Speaker—Spreading joy one smile at a time Social Media: www.sandyjoyweston.com
Awakening 17	Be Optimistic	**Sapan Shah** Energetic, Influential, and Motivator—Be Inspired and Be Result Driven
Awakening 18	Be Gritty	**Dr. Caren Baruch-Feldman** Psychologist and Author of *The Grit Guide for Teens: A Workbook to Help You Build Perseverance, Self-Control, and a Growth Mindset* Social Media: www.drbaruchfeldman.com

About the Author

Roopak Desai a Certified Applied Positive Psychology (CAPP) Practitioner, Coach, Mentor at iMentor, Leadership Coach at BRAVEN, Writer and Author. He participated in the first signature Habits and Happiness Program in 2012 conducted by The Institute of Advanced Human Performance (IFHAP). He has been a practitioner of meditation, mindfulness, and gratitude journaling since then. He now serves as a member coach at Positive Psychology led by Braco Pobric. Roopak's alter ego of a "MarathonForLife" runner after running helped him fight and negotiate anxiety and depression. And he shares how running is an ultimate way for practicing mindfulness meditation, which is the gateway to happiness, health, and sustained well-being. To date, he has run four full marathons, including the New York City marathon twice. He recently climbed Mount Kilimanjaro being fully present during the seven-day journey to the summit and back.

He lives in Monroe, New Jersey.

Contact Details:
Roopak Desai
Positive Psychology Practitioner, Coach, Writer, Author, and Motivational Speaker

Happiness, Well-Being, and High Performance
Cell: 848-248-1865,
E-mail: coachroopak@thecreativetransformations.com
Social Media: http://wwww.coachroopakdesai.com

34785026R10071

Made in the USA
Middletown, DE
02 February 2019